You Can Live
Stress-Free

You Can Live Stress-Free

by

Stephen Sumrall

You Can Live Stress-Free
ISBN 1-58568-206-3
Copyright © 2000 by Sumrall Publishing

Published by Sumrall Publishing
P. O. Box 12
South Bend, Indiana 46624

Contents

Contents

Introduction

You do not have to succumb to the modern-day disease of STRESS that permeates all levels of society. Stress is a killer, and Satan is the perpetrator of it. He delights in raising havoc in the Body of Christ, using STRESS as one of his vehicles. Once you understand how to resist it in the spiritual realm, you will overcome stress without adverse effects upon your life in the natural realm. You will discover that you can live stress-free!

As a young boy, we lived in Hong Kong for a period of time while Dr. Sumrall was starting New Life Temple Church. One day we read in the newspaper of a young boy who, not even ten years of age, went to the island side of Hong Kong and threw himself down off of an overpass to the street below to his death. He committed suicide because he could not stand up under the pressure that was put upon him to excel in all of his subjects at school, to go to college and then become the breadwinner for his entire family. Now, in the Western world, we don't understand this, but in the Orient particularly, that's just the way life is.

More recently, I read of a man who died of a heart attack a short time after becoming an instant millionaire by winning the lottery. He was inundated with people trying to get him to give them money. Charities were after him at all hours of the day and night. He was besieged by financial planners, accountants, lawyers, real estate agents and schemers, all wanting to help him invest his money. Before his sudden death, the only investment the man had time to make was to purchase a little dog for his son. His family said he could not handle the stress of all the people who pursued him to get their hands on his money. What a tragedy!

I'll tell you what, you don't have to bow your

knees to pressure and stress. It is the devil who wants your life to be meaningless. If he can heap enough garbage on you, he will keep you so overwhelmed that you are unable to do anything for the Kingdom of God. He wants to keep you under such a magnitude of stress that you just want to get through the grind of each day, praying for the night to come. Then in the night, you pray for daylight to come.

The good news is, God is the great Deliverer! In this book, I will share scriptural truths of how to overcome stress and live stress-free and be productive for God, throwing off the old garment of stress and putting on a new garment of freedom and joy.

Stephen Sumrall

1
Lacking in Godly Knowledge

Stress is a killer, and there are things we need to do to protect ourselves against it.

There is a saying that goes, Where there is slack, there will be lack. Proverbs 10:4 puts it this way: *He becometh poor that dealeth with a slack hand....* This is a person who isn't diligent and doesn't pay any attention to details. As a result, it gets him in trouble.

It is amazing, but it's not just the person in the pew who has to deal with stress. It's also the pastor, the evangelist and the missionary. Sometimes people in the pew have little understanding of the pressures that come against those in spiritual leadership. Some of these pressures are absolutely demonic, while others are self-inflicted.

There are professional ministers who study the Bible to get a sermon, and they could tell you in Greek and Hebrew what every word means, yet it is not their daily lifestyle to seek their manna from God's Word. They may go to the epistles to find a point for a sermon, but that is about all of the Bible reading they do. I'm telling you, whether you are a spiritual leader, a layman, or a laywoman, that will not sustain you in this day and age. It will not hold you close to the Lord.

Many of these same spiritual leaders do not have any kind of prayer life. Before they get in the pulpit, they might say, "God, help me," but that's about it.

If men of God, no matter what type of ministry they are in — and God's children regardless of their calling — would read and study the Word of God and pray as a daily habit, they would not experience lack in any area of their lives. If we would pursue the Word and prayer as much as we pursue coffee, tea, milk, or juice, or sit down and have breakfast, lunch and dinner, we would not succumb to the opportunities to be overcome with the pressures and stresses of life.

If you don't take time for the Word and prayer daily, when a situation or circumstances comes, you won't ask, "Lord, what do You want me to do?" Or, "Holy Spirit, guide me and direct me in the path that I should take." Suddenly, good people are making bad decisions that lead to stressful situations.

Lack Follows On the Heels of Slack

Where there is slack in your life, there will be lack. Where there is slack in your physical abilities and you don't have a proper regiment of exercise, diet and sleep, you will have a lack in your body. Where there is slack in watching over your income versus your expenses, there will be a lack in your finances.

With many people, there is slack in the appropriate use of their tongue. Their tongue becomes a blow torch that fires on people. It becomes a weapon to tear people apart. They have no idea how to control it. The problem is, they haven't read the book of James.

James tells us:

> *Even so the tongue is a little member, and boasteth great things. Behold, how great a matter a little fire kindleth!*
>
> *And the tongue is a fire, a world of iniquity: so is the tongue among our members, that it defileth the whole body, and setteth on fire the course of nature; and it is set on fire of hell.*
>
> (James 3:5-6)

If there is slack in your family, you need to spend more time with them. I have heard people say, "We have to have some quality family time, so we can't go to church on Sunday night." You'd better go to church on Sunday night with your family, because that is one of the best quality times you could ever have: bringing your family to the house of God; showing them how to pray; how to sing the songs of Zion; and how to pay attention to the servant of God who delivers God's Word. Only then will they learn how to apply these spiritual principles in practical ways in their lives.

If there is slack in your marriage relationship, there will be lack. If you don't pay attention to your wife, you don't talk to her, you barely grunt when you get up and don't even bother to say "Hi," "Bye," or anything else, there is going to be lack in that relationship. You are headed for trouble, and stress will develop.

Where there is slack in your life, there will be stress. When you didn't know about salvation, you were stressful. When something bad happens, you say, "Oh, my God, I'm going to die." Then all of a sudden, things get better and you forget God.

Then another tragedy happens and you say, "Oh, my, I'm going to die. God, I'm going to get right with You. What is going to happen to me, my family and my friends?" The spirit of fear comes all over you, and you have no idea how to handle it. Then stress walks right into your life big time!

If you don't know about healing, it is very easy to get stressful about it. Think of the woman with the issue of blood in Mark, chapter 5. She spent all she had on doctors and medicine and her condition was no better. At one point she was sick with money. Now she is sick and broke. That could have led to a very stressful life, but she had enough sense to get to Jesus. When she got to Jesus, she touched the hem of His garment and received her healing. The cause of stress in her life was gone.

When you don't know God's promises of provision, you will experience lack and stress in the financial area.

There is a verse in the book of Hosea that is quoted often: *My people are destroyed for lack of knowledge....* (Hosea 4:6). But people fail to finish the verse. It goes on, *...because thou hast rejected knowledge....* Sometimes people turn their backs on knowledge, because with knowledge comes responsibility. Few people want to be held accountable. Instead, they want to know only enough to make it through life.

Some people have stress in their lives because they have rejected the knowledge that is sitting right in front of their nose, particularly believers who are supposed to know the Word of God. They are supposed to know that Jesus Christ has come to set them free. They have willfully turned their backs on the knowledge of God, and as a result, have gotten themselves into all kinds of problems, and the killer disease, STRESS, has set in.

Hosea 4:6 goes on to say, *...because thou hast rejected knowledge [you have turned your back on God and on His ways], I will also reject thee, that thou shalt* *be no priest to me: seeing thou hast forgotten the law of thy God, I will also forget thy children."*

Isaiah chapter 5, verse 13, says it this way:

Therefore my people are gone into captivity, because they have no know-ledge: and their honourable men are famished, and their multitude dried up with thirst.

This speaks of the spiritual state of many churches and individuals today. "Honorable men" are those in leadership who know right. They know the Word of God. To be "famished" is to be weak and worn out. To be "dried up with thirst" means to be thirsty for more of God, for the things of God and for the miracles of God.

Time Alone With God

When there is lack, there will be stress. To get rid of the stressful situations in your life, you will need to take time out on a daily basis to get alone with God. This is so important in the modern, mechanized generation we live in.

Today we have "instant" everything — with phenomenal technology in phones, fax machines, pagers, you name it. The things of the Spirit of God, however, rarely come instantaneously. We think God should do everything *right now.* I've got news for you: *God doesn't have to do anything on our timetable!* He does things on His timetable.

It is up to us to cut ourselves loose from the cares of this world and decide, "I'm putting my spiritual foot down. I am following Jesus. I am going to spend time in the Word and in prayer." Then do it! Don't let anything tear you away from getting alone with God.

We can get so burned out just being in the ministry or as a layman or laywoman, just doing "good things," that we forget we are supposed to minister to God and worship Him. The stress we allow over our "good works" — teaching the Word, singing in the choir, teaching Sunday school, going to committee meetings, etc. — can be alleviated.

Stress is not from God. The first step to achieve victory over it is to *gain godly knowledge and become accountable to God for that which we do know.*

2
Filling Up On
the Word

When there is a lack in your life, one of the best things you can do is, *fill up on the Word of God.* As you fill up on the Word, you will begin to understand your authority as a son or a daughter of God. You will begin to understand that Jesus already defeated the devil for us, so now it's up to us to enforce that defeat.

I remember one brother, a grown man preparing for ministry, who was trying to discipline himself to take time each morning to get in the Word. He couldn't stay awake so he decided to read the Word while standing on the edge of his bathtub. He used to teeter and balance over the edge, with his heels on one side and his toes on the other. Needless to say, he learned to stay awake while reading the Word of God!

Another man, the head of a business, told his secretary, "I don't want to be bothered today. This is my day to read the Word of God."

Other people have shut themselves up in a room. Just like going to work and punching a clock, they commit a block of uninterrupted time to read the Word of God and pray, some for eight hours at a time. Other people have done this, in addition to having a regular, eight-hour-a-day job.

You may be thinking, "I can't do that. I have other responsibilities — the kids, the house, the washing, the dishes, etc." Start where you are. There is no condemnation in that.

Don't despise the day of small beginnings. You can start out reading the Word of God for five minutes. Or, if you can shut yourself away with God for half an hour, do it. I'm not advocating every single person to take eight hours or even a full day to spend in the Word and in prayer, but I am saying, "do as much as you possibly can to get the Word inside of you."

What's Coming Out of Your Mouth?

Whether we realize it or not, all of us are "confession" people, because Matthew 12:34 says, *...out of the abundance of the heart the mouth speaketh.*

There are some negative connotations about the so-called "confession group," because of the people who have been out of balance and all mixed up with methodology. For example, we've all heard, "I'm going to have a Cadillac because I've confessed for it." Sad to say, we have gotten this confession thing completely out of joint, and people are confessing things that are non-scriptural. We are to be confessors of the Word of God — not confessors of man-made dreams, opinions and negatives.

An example of a Word-based confession is in the salvation experience. The Bible says we must confess with the mouth that Jesus Christ is Lord and believe in our heart that God raised Him from the dead, then we will be saved (Romans 10:9,10).

The same principle is true with healing. We agree with what the Word of God says: *By Jesus' stripes I am healed* (1 Peter 2:24). *Jesus took my infirmities, and bore my sicknesses* (Matthew 8:17). That is the type of confession I am talking about.

If there is doubt and fear on the inside of you, you will confess doubt and fear. If there is failure on the inside of you, then words of failure will come out of your mouth. If the flu is going around and you are saying, "The flu is going to get me," it will find its way to you all right.

If you are saying, "My children are going to run away from home; they are going to be drug addicts, alcoholics and criminals," what you confess is what you'll get. Whether you realize it or not, you are confessing good or bad with every single word that you speak.

Some people say, "Healing doesn't work for me." That's right, it won't work for you because you just said, "It does not work for me."

Your words, whether good or bad, positive or

negative, will actually set your destiny (good or bad) in motion: "I'm never going to get ahead in life." "I'm always going to be down under." "I'm always going to be on this side of the railroad tracks." Friend, that is exactly where you will be.

In order to destroy stress in your life, you must change the way you talk and line your words up with what God says about you in His Word.

You Will Be Known By Your Fruit

In Matthew, chapter 12, Jesus had just cast the devil out of a person who was blind and dumb. The religious Pharisees rose up and accused Jesus of casting out devils *...by Beelzebub the prince of the devils* (v. 24). Jesus let them know that was an impossibility because *...Every kingdom ...city or house divided against itself shall not stand* (v. 25).

Jesus goes on in verses 31-33:

...All manner of sin and blasphemy shall be forgiven unto men: but the blasphemy against

the Holy Ghost shall not be forgiven unto men.

And whosoever speaketh a word against the Son of man, it shall be forgiven him: but whosoever speaketh against the Holy Ghost, it shall not be forgiven him, neither in this world, neither in the world to come.

Either make the tree good, and his fruit good; or else make the tree corrupt, and his fruit corrupt: <u>for the tree is known by his fruit</u>.

The point I want to emphasize is, just as a tree is known by its fruit, your life is known by the people you hang around with, the people you associate with, the ones you compare notes with, joke with, lunch with, work with and vacation with. Some people say, "My friends can't drag me down." Yes, they can. If you can't lift them up, they can drag you down. Jesus is saying, "A believer will be known by his or her fruit, not by what he or she says."

Many people inside the house of God know all the right protocol — when to stand, when to sit, what song to sing and some can even quote Scripture verbatim — but *the fruit on the tree of their life speaks louder than what they say.* The fruit on the tree of their life, while at the warehouse dock on Monday morning, speaks louder than what they spoke on Sunday.

We are creating our own stress when we refuse to watch what we say. A good tree or a corrupt tree is known by its fruit.

Second Corinthians 3:2 says, *Ye are our epistle written in our hearts, known and read of all men.* You can't disguise yourself. What is going on inside of you is going to come out sooner or later. If you are full of stress, it will come out.

Out of the mouth of a positive person, you may hear: "This is going to be a great day. I know that this is going wrong, but I tell you what, by the end of the day, things will turn around. It is going to be better."

Out of the mouth of a negative person, you may hear: "This is going to be a lousy day. Things are tough and hard. This is coming up and that is coming up. I know God is not going to answer our prayer. It's just going to be a bad day. In fact, I should have stayed in bed."

Sometimes people know you better than you do. Of course, God knows us inside and out, topside and bottomside. Sometimes we think we are fooling people. You're not fooling anyone. You might wear a mask to disguise your emotions or your heart, but sooner or later what is inside is going to surface. You are going to reveal what you really are inside by the words you speak. We are living epistles.

In Matthew 12:34, Jesus continues:

O generation of vipers, how can ye, being evil, speak good things? for out of the abundance of the heart the mouth speaketh.

Out of the abundance of your heart, you will speak. The facade of a person under pressure is going to be blown away. This is what has happened to so many believers in the last few years. Hard times have come and the facade is gone.

Out of the abundance of their heart filth and garbage are bubbling up to the surface, overflowing and spewing out. They can't disguise it anymore. They have created their own stressful situations because of things that are deep inside of them, which they have not allowed God to deal with.

Putting Good Treasure in Your Heart

Jesus goes on in verse 35 of Matthew chapter 12:

A good man out of the <u>good treasure</u> of the heart bringeth forth good things....

How do we get the *good treasure*? By making continual installments of the Word of God and prayer. ...and an evil man out of the evil treasure bringeth forth evil things (v. 35). Either you are bringing forth good treasure or evil treasure every single day. The key to bringing forth good treasure is to *keep making daily deposits of God's Word in your treasury* (your heart).

Everyone faces some tough times and stressful situations, but how you react to these adverse circumstances depends on what has been deposited in your heart. How are you going to react when the transmission goes out? When the house is on fire? When the kids run away? Or when you get fired from your job? Are you going to be under duress, stress and fear? It all depends on what kinds of things you have been depositing in your heart and in your mind. Have you been meditating on soap operas, novels and stories that exist only in the fabrication of someone's mind, or on God's Word?

When you get buffeted a little bit by the devil, what do you do? Do you fold up your tent and move away? Or, do you say, "No, sir, in Jesus' name, I've been putting the Word of God in my heart. I've been putting prayer into my life. I am going to stand up against this attack in the mighty name of Jesus. I will not succumb to the stress of this situation. I will stand up in the face of the storm, and like Jesus did 2,000 years ago, I am going to say, 'Peace, be still,' not because of who I am, a mere human being, but because of the One to whom I belong!"

If your treasury is filled with God's Word, you can speak to the storms, to the poverty, to the kids and to the sickness. You can command the calm of God into your situations and simply refuse to bow your knee to stress. Stress is a killer, and it can rob you of your joy, and cause you to be sour on life, sour on God, sour on the church — sour on everything and everyone.

The enemy's purpose is to attack you, hurt you and defeat you. You must defend yourself against him *by filling your heart and your mouth with the Word of God.*

To fill your heart with God's positive words of healing, reproof, rebuke and correction will cut the stress out of your life to where, when you come up against a negative situation, you will know exactly what to say and what to do. The Holy Spirit will bring the Word that is inside of you back to your remembrance.

3
Crying Unto the Lord

We can't allow ourselves to buckle under stress, because when we do, the devil will put his foot on our neck and grind us into the dirt, which is exactly what he wants to do.

When faced with problems or stressful situations, some say, "I don't know what I'm going to do." Or, "I am going to see my banker. Maybe he can give me a loan." Or, "I'm going to go to the psychiatrist. Maybe he can straighten me out." Or, "I'm going to go to my barber or to the next-door neighbor. Maybe they will know what to do for my problem."

Many of these people have absolutely no idea what motivates a person to do what he or she does. While they may understand the science of the mind, they don't understand the spirit of man at all. They have no idea what to do, so you need to *cry unto the Lord*. You need to slam the door shut in the face of the enemy and say, "No, you don't, in Jesus' name. You can't come into my house, into my mind, or into my body."

For some of us, when we hear the little knock at the door, we say, "Sickness, is that you?" Sickness answers, "Yes, here I am." And sometimes we say, "I've been looking for you. Come on in." That might sound foolish, but that's the way we act sometimes. Some people say, "I hear the Hong Kong flu is going around. I might get it. My kids might get it. We may have to take off two or three weeks from work just to recuperate," and it hasn't arrived yet!

At other times, failure, confusion, or disappointment may knock on our door. Instead of keeping the door closed, we open it a crack and say, "Who's out there?" You don't have to talk to the devil. Just keep the door closed and yell through it, "No, you don't, devil. You can't come into my house or into my life, in Jesus' name."

There is an old saying, especially in the Middle East, that when a camel gets its nose in your tent, just be prepared to move out because the rest of that camel is going to come inside. That's the way it is with the enemy. When he gets his toe in your doorway, the rest of him is going to come in *if you don't protect your home.* How do you do that? By what you allow in your home through the radio, TV, cassettes, CD's, records, tapes and videos.

You have to protect your home from what is brought into it by your spouse, visitors and your kids. You have to be watchful over what you hear. If you hear gossip and you repeat it, just like participation in any other sin, it will open the door to the enemy and his destructive plots against your life, marriage and family.

Just Cry Unto the Lord!

Psalm 107:28 says, *Then they cry unto the Lord in their trouble, and he bringeth them out of their distresses.* There is a release from stress when you cry unto the Lord in the time of trouble. He will bring you out of distress. Maybe you are in a distressful situation right now and you have cried to everybody *except the Lord.*

If you want true deliverance, not just relief, you can break through and destroy the devil's stranglehold that is on your life. Personally, I do not want temporary relief. I want to be set free from it, in the mighty name of Jesus.

Take a stand by making a decision and putting your foot down, "No, devil, you cannot come into my house. You cannot come into my life. Take your distress and go right now, in the name of Jesus."

Ephesians 6:13,14 says, ...having done all, to stand. Stand therefore.... *Fight the enemy with the sword of the Spirit, which is the Word of God, and you will win over stress. You can live a stress-free life.*

You're <u>Not</u> Doomed to the Valley!

Let's look at Psalm 23 from *The Amplified Bible.* I want to emphasize verse 4.

The Lord is my Shepherd [to feed, guide, and shield me], I shall not lack.

He makes me to lie down in [fresh, tender] green pastures; He leads me beside the still and restful waters.

He refreshes and restores my life (my self); He leads me in the paths of righteousness [uprightness and right standing with Him — not for my earning it, but] for His name's sake.

Yes, though I <u>walk through</u>....

(Verses 1-4)

That's the key, friend. You don't have to camp in the valley of the shadow of death where stress drags you down to where you hate to see the sun come up or the sun go down; where you hate to go to work and you hate to come back home; where you don't want to eat or you can't stop eating.

We hear the saying, "I'm all stressed out." That means, "I am so beyond myself that I don't know what to do. I'm at the end of my rope."

Yes, though I walk through the [deep, sunless] valley of the shadow of death... (v. 4).

Don't camp in the valley of the shadow of death. Walk through it, in Jesus' name. Where there are shadows, at least there is evidence of light! Keep walking towards that light, and you will come out of that valley, in Jesus' name.

Maybe you are in a deep valley of despair right now, and you don't know how in the world to get out. You have no idea of how to escape the situation you are in. You are saying, "God, where do I turn? I guess I am destined to be in this long, dark, lonesome valley the rest of my life." No, you're not! You don't have to camp in that valley.

God Is Right There With You!

Verse 4 goes on to say:

> *...I will fear or dread no evil, for <u>You are with me</u>....*

Many times when you get into a stressful situation, the devil will lie to you, and say, "God doesn't care. He's not listening or paying any attention to you, so stop crying out to Him. Stop believing God, because you are wasting your time."

Don't be deceived by the devil, because verse

4 says <u>God is with you</u>! God is with you in the valley and on the mountaintop. Whether you are shouting "Hallelujah!" praising God and having a great time in church, or you are all alone and all your earthly friends are gone, God is in the same place. <u>He is right there with you</u>!

Verse 4 goes on:

> *...Your rod [to protect] and Your staff [to guide], they comfort me.*

You can receive comfort from the Holy Spirit today. You can receive comfort from God to where you are not troubled, disappointed, or upset.

Revelation 1:18 says,

> *"I am he that liveth, and was dead; and, behold, I am alive for evermore, Amen; and have the keys of hell and of death."*

When you cry out to God, don't cry out in despair, but cry out in faith: "You are Abba Father. You have complete ability to heal me and set me free." When you realize this, you will be set free of the stress you are experiencing. Revelation 1:18 reveals that <u>God is God</u>! He is the

One Who has enough power and ability to set you free from every lie and stressor of the devil.

David, the psalmist, said,

> *The Lord is my light and my salvation; whom shall I fear? the Lord is the strength of my life; of whom shall I be afraid?*

(Psalm 27:1)

What a fantastic scripture! Because God is on your side and Jesus is your Lord, there should not be room for any stress in your life.

When you cry unto the Lord and you realize Who He is — your Father God, the omnipotent God, the all-powerful God — the circumstances and problems around you will shrink.

Some people say, "God, take a look at my mountain." Instead, you should be saying, "Mountain, take a look at my God!"

4

Passing a Faith Test

Many people want to have a testimony without going through a test or a battle. They want to sing songs about victory, but you can't sing a song about victory until you take your sword out, swing it and hit *the enemy* — not your brothers and sisters in the Lord! (Some of our problem is that we have fought one another rather than the enemy.)

As a shepherd boy, David was elevated above King Saul for defeating Goliath. David could not have received the adulation, ...*Saul hath slain his thousands, and David his ten thousands* (1 Samuel 18:7), if he had not been bold enough to go out and fight Goliath and the armies that were against God.

All during the time he was a shepherd, David fed on the Word of God. When he faced the giant, who was almost ten feet tall, he knew inside of himself, "This problem is not too big for my God," just like the lion and the bear weren't too big for Him! Regardless of your circumstances or problems, *the challenges you are facing right now are not bigger than your God!*

Count It All Joy!

Some people want to wear the armor of victory without a fight. James, chapter 1, verse 2, tells us we are in a warfare. My brethren, count it all joy when ye fall into divers [or various] temptations. We can count it all joy when we realize the power of God is going to help us overcome the temptation, test, or trial. We can count it all joy because our God is sufficient. We can count it all joy when we lean on His arm of strength. We can count it all joy when we know we are going to be the victor.

When two football teams start running at each other, they don't know who is going to win. Sometimes there is a fumble, an interception, or the sacking of the quarter-back that turns the tide of the game. Then one team is victorious over the other.

Seemingly, for the whole game, they can butt heads just like bulls and hit each other with no ground gained. But one little mistake by one team and the game goes in the opposite direction, and the winner is determined.

I tell you we can go into divers kinds of temptations, trials and all kinds of warfare and know that we are winners. God already made us winners. Jesus Christ's defeat of Satan at the Cross!

Adding Patience to Your Faith

James 1:2,3 in The Amplified says:

Consider it wholly joyful, my brethren, whenever you are enveloped in or encounter trials of any sort or fall into various temptations.

Be assured and understand that the trial and the proving of your faith bring out endurance and steadfastness and patience.

When you are in a stressful situation and you have an opportunity either to flip out or to have faith, that is the "trying of your faith" to see what kind of metal you are made of. Don't look at stress as your enemy, but as an opportunity to gain a victory in the name of Jesus — to show His strength to this generation and to show the devil that he is not in charge!

Many people are up and down or on and off in their faith. When we talk about a runner who has endurance, that means he can go the long haul. That's what we need in Christendom today, people who aren't hot for God one minute and cold the next.

> *...the trying of your faith worketh patience."*
> (James 1:3)

The more trials and battles in your life, the stronger your faith will become.

The natural response of most people is, "I don't want the trials, temptations, testings and battles." Then you are not going to be a strong believer. You will be weak, wishy washy, up and down. With every attack of the enemy, pressure and stress will come. If you are weak in faith, you will throw up your hands and say, "I can't cope with this. What in the world do I do now?"

The things that come against you are opportunities to bring endurance to your faith and victory to your testimony. Praise God!

Purified By Fire!

Steel is made perfect when it is thrust into the fire and beat on with an anvil. That's the way our faith is. God is constantly working with us, thrusting us into the fire, taking His sledgehammer and gently beating us on one side and on the other. It's not a painful situation, but He is shaping us and forming us. The same procedure is true with gold. The Bible tells us that there is a refiner's fire for gold and silver, where the heat is so hot that it is almost white hot — so hot that it incinerates anything in its pathway. That's when pure gold comes to the forefront. (The impurities aren't going to leave if the fire is lukewarm.) That is exactly what God wants to do in our lives.

We have to realize that sometimes it is painful in the fire, but it removes the impurities. God is working on our faith. The *working of our faith* develops patience, pure gold, silver and steel so we can combat things such as stress.

James 1:4 says, *"But let patience have her perfect work, that ye may be perfect and entire, wanting nothing." James is still talking about the perfecting of our faith.*

This verse in *The Amplified* reads:

> But let endurance and steadfastness and patience have full play and do a thorough work, so that you may be [people] perfectly and fully developed [with no defects], lacking in nothing.

> God wants our faith to be perfect and fully developed with no defects, lacking absolutely nothing.

Ask for Wisdom

> *"If any of you lack wisdom, let him ask of God, that*

*giveth to all men liberally, and upbraideth not; and it shall
be given him"*

(James 1:5)

In other words, God has an answer for every single question or dilemma in our lives.

Ask of God and He will give you wisdom. Don't allow stressful situations, problems and failures to pile up, one on top of the other. There is an old proverbial saying, "It's the little straw that breaks the camel's back." There is a saturation point where just one more straw is one too many, and it breaks down the entire system. It's not just your children leaving the bicycle out in the middle of the sidewalk, but it's all the other little things that have happened during the day that push you over the edge.

God is telling us to patiently work on our faith. Patiently have the endurance that is needed. Don't let those things upset you. If you can't do it with the help of the Word of God and your brothers and sisters in the Lord, just go ahead and ask God, because He will give His wisdom to you liberally. He wants to give you good things so you will experience continual victories in your life.

Unwavering Faith

> *But let him ask in faith, nothing wavering. For he that wavereth is like a wave of the sea driven with the wind and tossed.*
>
> James 1:6

We are to ask in faith that has stood the test of time, that has had endurance added to it, that has been tested in the fire and had all the impurities burned out.

If you have weak faith, you are going to lose out, but if you have faith that has been tested and tried and is true to God, you are not going to waver. You are going to stand on the Word of God and receive God's answers to your prayers.

Dr. Sumrall used to say, "You can't ask God for a seven-tier cake when you haven't even asked Him for a cupcake yet!" Our faith can grow when we have a greater knowledge of God and a greater understanding of His Word.

You have to start where you are at. Don't begin by saying, "Oh, God, I need $1 million. You might need $1 million, but have you found out that God is faithful with $100? Or $1,000? "Oh, God, I want to save the whole world." That's wonderful to have the desire, but have you brought your loved ones to the Lord?

Or, "God, I want to go to India, Africa and China, and preach to the masses." Have you gone down to the street corner and passed out tracts to two or three people?

Christian growth is a process, not a recession. It is a growth in faith and in the knowledge of God that will take you from victory to victory — from a smaller victory to a bigger victory, to an even bigger victory. That's what God wants in our lives.

God is not interested in quick fixes. He is interested in developing you and me, *"Till we all come in the unity of the faith, and of the knowledge of the Son of God, unto a perfect man, unto*

the measure of the stature of the fulness of Christ"
(Ephesians 4:13).

5

Getting the Mind of God

To overcome stress and live in continual victory, you must *get the mind of God, put it in gear and then into practice.*

Many people have gone to church for years, and they have heard the Word of God time after time. They know so much, but they do so little as far as witnessing. They say, "I can't witness to anybody. I'm shy. I don't know what to say." Or, "I am going to meet up with a Muslim or someone in a cult, and they are going to argue with me. I won't know what to say."

Although they have been in the church for many years, they still don't know the Word of God. Their Bible has been opened only on Sundays in church. It remains closed the rest of the time. The Word won't work for you until you get it into your home on a daily basis. For generations people have been getting the mind of God. Although they have heard teaching of the Word through seminars, books and tapes, they have put little, if any, into practice.

Just Do It!

In 1 Chronicles 28:20, we have a conversation between David and Solomon. David, a mighty warrior, wanted to build the temple of God. But because his hands were bloody from war, God would not allow him to build His temple. God told David that He would allow his son Solomon to build His temple.

Verse 20 of 1 Chronicles 28 says:

> *And David said to Solomon his son, Be strong and of good courage, <u>and do it</u>...."*

I have seen motivational posters and plaques that say, "Just do it." In the business realm, this means, "Don't procrastinate. Don't let your competition get the jump on you. Just get in there and do it."

In the spirit realm, we need to say to ourselves,

"Just do it." We've got umpteen Bibles and tapes, and we've been seminared until we are saturated with God's Word. All we have to do is obey it and put it into practice!

In this day and age, we have unprecedented opportunities to go to the world to preach the Gospel of Jesus Christ. All kinds of curtains are falling down and all kinds of walls are being demolished. Today, you can publish the Good News that Jesus is real and He is alive in places where, in previous years, it was restricted. Now, you can go in these same areas and guards will smile and wave at you as you go by. Several countries are saying, "Come and teach us. We want the Bibles, the seminars, the tapes and everything you've got." They devour the Word of God and are taking their nations for God, in the mighty name of Jesus.

I believe the Lord is telling us, *just do it*. You have the information, the tools and the ability. Now is the time to *just do it*.

Fear Not!

After David encouraged Solomon to be strong and of good courage, he said: *"...fear not, nor be dismayed: for the Lord God, even my God, will be with thee...."* (1 Chronicles 28:20). That is absolutely dynamite! This is what God is speaking to us today.

The greatest tool the enemy uses against us is this thing called *fear*. Fear of the unknown, fear of witnessing, fear of praying for someone, thinking nothing will happen — as if we've got anything to do with it anyway!

Jesus was bruised, He was whipped, He wore the crown of thorns upon His head for the whole of humanity. That's part of this stress thing. We take the weight of the whole world upon our shoulders like we are personally responsible for the salvation of who is headed for hell, or for the healing and deliverance of those who are sick and oppressed.

Our responsibility is to be a channel of the

blessings of God and of His anointing. We don't control God's power. God is just using us as available tools. He is using people from other churches and ethnic groups, too. When we cease to be available tools or we start taking credit for some of the things being done by His Spirit, He is going to cut us off cold and move on to someone else who will move with Him.

It is totally God's mercy that allows us the privilege to flow in His anointing and be channels of blessing to others. It is because of what Jesus did on the Cross — not because of our ability or who we are.

When Your Back Is Up Against the Wall, Rehearse Past Victories!

God has never failed or forsaken His people. Old Testament prophets reminded God of some of His previous accomplishments when their backs were against the wall: "God, don't You remember how You took Israel from Egypt into the promised land? Don't You remember how this army or that army came and You defeated them?"

Sometimes the problems can be mounted so high that we forget what God has done in the past. What God has done before, He will do again and again and again. He says in His Word, *"For I am the Lord, I change not..."* (Malachi 3:6). God does not change. His ability does not change. His character does not change. His will does not change. He is the same yesterday, today and forever (Hebrews 13:8).

The scriptural account of Joshua and his fighting men taking Jericho is an example of a "super-natural plan" — making little or no sense in the natural — that overcame the enemy. In fact, this is an awesome victory. Let's look briefly at this account in Joshua 6:1-5,15,16,20 AMP:

> *Now Jericho [a fenced town with high walls] was tightly closed because of the Israelites; no one went out or came in.*
>
> *And the Lord said to Joshua, See I have given Jericho, its king and mighty men of valor, into your hands.*

You shall march around the enclosure, all the men of war going around the city once. This you shall do for six days.

And seven priests shall bear before the ark seven trumpets of rams' horns; and on the seventh day you shall march around the enclosure seven times, and the priests shall blow the trumpets.

When they make a long blast with the ram's horn and you hear the sound of the trumpet, all the people shall shout with a great shout; and the wall of the enclosure shall fall down in its place and the people shall go up [over it], every man straight before him...

On the seventh day they rose early at daybreak and marched around the city as usual, only on that day they compassed the city seven times.

And the seventh time, when the priests had blown the trumpets, Joshua said to the people, Shout! For the Lord has given you the city...

So the people shouted, and the trumpets were blown. When the people heard the sound of the trumpet, they raised a great shout, and [Jericho's] wall fell down in its place, so that the [Israelites] went up into the city, every man straight before him, and they took the city.

In the natural, Joshua and his men should have been full of fear, but they were fearless because they knew what God had spoken, what He had done in the past, and they knew He would do it again. That's why they could *go for it!*

We are serving the same God Who knows exactly what we are going through. He knows how to meet every single crisis in our lives. Just as David spoke to Solomon, God is speaking to you and me to be strong and courageous. Confess the Word of God. Allow your faith to be purified in the flames. Go up against insurmountable odds, because it is the power of God in us that will bring victory *every time!*

God will never fail or forsake us. He is not going to leave this generation to flounder on their own. The Bible says He is coming back for a Bride without spot or wrinkle, who is strong, bold in the Word of God and true to the very end. I hope you are saying, "That's me!"

Don't let the stress of the devil or the things of this world heap burdens on you. You're not the Burden-bearer. Jesus is the Burden-bearer. Keep that in mind. God is on your side, and He is lifting you up to new heights, in Jesus' name. Amen.

MY CHALLENGE TO YOU

Have you received Jesus Christ as the Lord of your life? If your life were to end today, would you be able to stand before God with the confidence that your sins were forgiven? If you are not sure, I invite you to receive Jesus as your Savior now. Please pray:

"Dear Lord Jesus, I am a sinner. I do believe that you died and rose from the dead to save me from my sins. I want to be with you in heaven forever. God, forgive me of all my sins that I have committed against you. I here and now open my heart to you and ask you to come into my heart and life and be my personal Savior. Amen."

When you pray the Sinner's Prayer and mean it, He will come in instantly. You are now a child of God and you have been transferred from the devil's dominion to the kingdom of God. Read 1 John 1:9 and Colossians 1:13.

If you have prayed this prayer, we would like to hear what Jesus has done for you. We will send you a pamphlet entitled, "So You're Born Again." Mail your letter to:

STEPHEN SUMRALL
P.0. Box 12
South Bend, IN 46624

About LeSEA Global Feed The Hungry

LeSEA Global Feed The Hungry was created in 1987 to feed the hungry around the world and provide emergency relief to those in need as a result of famine, drought, flood, war or other disasters. Our mission is simple . . . to show God's compassion to people in need, to bless "forgotten" members within the body of Christ, to strengthen the church and evangelize the lost. We are a pastor to pastor, church to church program by which supplies are given to leaders within the church or church community who in turn give to those experiencing need.

Why is LeSEA Global Feed The Hungry so dedicated to the poor and hurting? One reason is because there is great need in our world. It is estimated that one billion people (most of whom are children) live in hunger. However, the primary motive for our dedication is obedience to the Word of God. Those who have this world's goods are instructed to bless those who have not (1 Timothy 6:17-19).

"It wasn't by accident that I was awakened at midnight in Jerusalem in 1987. God wanted to speak to me. He let me know that Christians who had no food were praying, 'give us this day or daily bread.' Our efforts are simply to put bread in their mouths."

Lester Sumrall

LESEA Feed the Hungry
PO Box 12
South Bend, IN 46624

www.feedthehungry. org

About the Author

Dr. Stephen Sumrall is a powerful and anointed speaker and author with a compassionate heart for the lost and needy souls of the world. He has served as president of LeSEA Ministries for 20 years. In addition to heading the multi-faceted LeSEA, Inc., he is the senior pastor of Christian Center Cathedral of Praise in South Bend, Indiana, hosts two daily television programs, "New World Harvest," and "Storming The Gates." He also ministers extensively overseas. Together with their five beautiful children, Stephen and his wife Diane reside in South Bend, Indiana.

TAPES BY STEPHEN SUMRALL

- *THE CHARACTER OF JESUS CHRIST*
(Two-tape video set)

- *WORDS AND ATTITUDES*
(Four-tape audio set)

For a list of other books and tapes
by Dr. Stephen Sumrall,
please write to:

Sumrall Publishing
P.O. Box 12, South Bend, IN 46624
1-888-584-4847
www.sumrallpublishing.com